AF413584

HOW TO MANAGE YOUR MANAGER?

HOW TO MANAGE YOUR MANAGER?

A REFERENCE GUIDE FOR GROWTH IN TODAY'S PROFESSIONAL WORLD

SAKTI BAGCHI

Notion Press

Old No. 38, New No. 6
McNichols Road, Chetpet
Chennai - 600 031

First Published by Notion Press 2017
Copyright © Sakti Bagchi 2017
All Rights Reserved.

ISBN

Paperback 978-1-946983-22-0

Hardcase 979-8-89519-217-7

Dedication

To all my managers who have supported and encouraged me
to believe in myself.

Illustrations by super talented cartoonist
Nandakumar Shenoy who is an accomplished
manager himself.

Contents

SIMPLE MANTRA..!

Preface

L anding a software job when the dot-com crash made many software engineers jobless was a major life event for me. After barely making it, I was then faced with the challenge of being accepted by well-established professionals who did not think I was a good fit for professional world.

There were several instances in my early career when I had put all my efforts in the right direction, but a close associate was given credit for my endeavors, and I was ignored. My mistakes were highlighted, but my good deeds were forgotten. I had a terrible struggle with communicating with most people as well. At times, my thick vernacular accent got on the way. On other occasions, my desire to be certain of facts before I spoke with somebody senior blocked me from expressing myself freely.

Fortunately, during the early phase of this struggle, I realized that I had to work on fixing this issue. Hence, I started experimenting with different, small ways of influencing others, getting my points across and making friends. I was successful in my first few attempts. I continued doing the same, and soon, I overcame my blocker.

In no time, the world seemed turned around for me. I started receiving acceptance from my colleagues. This journey continued. I worked with different teams and managers for over one and a half decades of my career. My stand as an independent, confident professional continued achieving what I wanted with hardly any hurdle. Many people asked me, "What's your secret? You seem to get along with every colleague and manager and to continue growing in your career." I usually answer, "I know how to manage my manager."

Acknowledgments

I pray to God for the good health of my parents. They made me what I am, and their teaching is still the most relevant one in my life.

NANDA

Introduction

This nonfiction book is illustrated with fictitious events. The other two characters (Anuj and Siddharth) and the situations are imaginary, but how these two guys think and speak is no different from the way you and I do. My service in software companies throughout my career has influenced the core of this book to be mostly applicable to employees in the software industry, but my discussions with friends in other industries have made me believe that it is not much different in other sectors.

If you purchased this ebook, thinking that it would include a secret trick that you could use as a magic wand to control your boss, then I highly recommend that you request for a refund. Nevertheless, it will help you *manage your manager*. Managing your manager's perception, behavior, and attitude toward you through systematic changes in your own behavior and attitude is what this book is really all about.

The fictional aspects of this book take place against the backdrop of a beautiful Indian city called Vadodara or Baroda. I have chosen Baroda because it has influenced me to try my luck in the writing world. I also confess that I have not used all the methods mentioned in this book myself but have observed positive results when others have applied the strategies in their careers.

I am confident that reading through all the different techniques will empower you to rapidly progress in your professional career.

Award ceremony

CONGRATULATIONS ON YOUR 20-YEAR ANNIVERSARY!
YOU ARE A MYSTERY
SECRET ?
NANDA

The hustle and bustle on the floor diverted my attention from my work. I looked at my watch, and the time explained the distraction. It was 4 p.m. In all offices in India, this is the time when people pause from their work to take a tea break. I always wondered why 4 p.m. was the preferred time for a break, but wondering is not worth the investment when freshly prepared Indian tea is in front of you.

Today seemed a bit unusual, as I found that everyone was walking toward the large cafeteria on the terrace. Usually, people preferred to pick up a cup of tea and gather in the open spaces on the floor to have a chat.

Anuj came to me and said, "Let's go to the cafeteria!" I did not question him but walked along with him. When we reached the cafeteria, the scene was not what I had expected. The projector screen displayed my photo with a congratulatory note below it: "Congratulations on your 20-year anniversary!"

I knew it was coming but had no idea that the management and the staff would celebrate it with such grandeur. Despite my aptitude on stage, I would get a little nervous when seeing many people looking at me. Thus, I just walked across the cafeteria and stopped at a corner to see what would unfold.

Many of my previous managers spoke about me and made me feel good with their kind words. Many of the people who reported to me previously or currently also spoke nicely about me. It all felt good but monotonous.

Surprisingly, Siddharth, who had worked with me several years ago, took the stage. We had hardly interacted in recent years. I listened carefully to hear what he would say. He started, "Sakti, you are a mystery. How can you survive for 20 years in a single company? What's the secret?"

I was called to the stage to speak about my journey. Keeping my speech short, I thanked everyone for their help and support.

The ceremony ended soon after our president handed over a memento and a gift certificate.

At the end of the day, I met Siddharth in the elevator. Looking at me, he said, "Sakti, you did not answer my question."

I smiled and asked him to join Anuj and me the next day at 5 a.m. at a tea shop close to the office. He agreed. I could see curiosity in his eyes. I asked, "Are you a morning person?"

He replied, "I am. I usually go jogging at that time but never mind. I shall be there."

What's your business?

YOUR MANAGERS ARE YOUR CUSTOMERS
CASH
2017
NANDA

"You are very lucky! You got everything that you deserved at the right time," Anuj roared excitedly.

For most people, 5:00 a.m. is a time to continue sleeping, but many health-conscious people use it for exercising. Irrespective of the activity that a person chooses to engage in, nobody gets into any intense discussion at that time.

I was with Anuj at Shiva's Tea Shop, which was already open at that time to attract morning passersby along Dr. Vikram Sarabhai Road. Anuj came specifically to meet me and discuss the recent organizational changes that had placed him under a new manager. Since the beginning of our conversation that morning, he had been talking about how I enjoyed favorable work conditions while he did not. I was mostly quiet; I understood that Anuj was venting his frustration and not really looking for answers.

Siddharth joined us and quietly listened to our conversation. Anuj continued to prod me, seeking my opinion about the ways of dealing with his manager's rude behavior.

I could see that Siddharth was getting irritated with him. Siddharth said, "I don't understand why you care about your manager so much. Be the way you are, and it should be the manager's job to understand you so that he can get the work done. He is there because of the team, not the other way around. I hate your kind of submissive attitude, Anuj."

"It is easy to say that, Siddharth, when you don't have any career goals," countered Anuj. "You have been in the same position for seven years, and your peers are now better placed than you—Kishore is now an architect, and Samar just moved out on a foreign assignment. They are both earning more than you and have more respect for the organization. Are they better than you in any respect? No!"

Extremely upset, Siddharth blurted out, "I can't do buttering. I can't please somebody under false pretenses just to get my job done or to advance in my career. I will speak only the truth and do what is right. If others don't like what I say, I don't care. It's their problem. I am sure that one day, I will be recognized. Attention-seeking, unethical managers don't deserve my kindness. I am safe as long as I am doing a good job."

Anuj turned his attention to me, expecting some expert comment. I had been his manager three years ago, and we were close friends despite his being more than a decade younger than me.

"Do you see how Shiva handles his customers? He does not serve tea as soon as a customer arrives, but when tea is ready. He makes tea for ten people when he sees at least five or six customers. It must be tough for him to dictate his ways to clients in this competitive world. Why would anybody wait for him to prepare tea? People could go to the next tea shop, which has a great ambiance," I said.

Anuj answered, "But the flavor of the tea in this place is unmatchable. People who come here know that they may have to wait for 10 to 15 minutes, but they don't mind the delay."

"Have you observed that he behaves so nicely with all his customers and personally serves tea to his frequent customers?" Siddharth asked.

Just then, Shiva came to serve our tea and sat next to us. "So, sir! How are you all?" he greeted us.

"We are fine, Shiva. Thank you!" I said.

We have been discussing how well you run your business, Shiva," I added.

"If it is your business, then you must run it well. Who else will run it for you?" Shiva said.

"Unfortunately, we are not into business. We, the members of the serving class, are meant to remain at the mercy of others," Anuj said.

Shiva protested, "I am sorry, but you've got your business completely wrong, sir! We are all running a business. I am selling tea; you are selling your knowledge. You are all my customers. Your managers are your customers. My customers pay and give me more opportunities to serve if they are happy with me. Your managers must be giving you better work or rewards when they are satisfied with your work and confident about your deliverables. So we are all in business. To do your business well, you have to understand what business you are in. More importantly, understand your customers." He saw some new customers coming and knew that it was time to prepare another round of tea, so he excused himself.

Anuj and Siddharth were in deep thought.

"So, friends, is it always luck that helps you succeed in your career? This thought itself is enough to make you question your job, irrespective of the business you are in. Just think of what Shiva said. Understand your business and customers. Then think about how to run your business well. Some guidance on how to identify and manage your manager may be beneficial," I said.

Anuj immediately corrected me. "Identify your customer and manage your manager."

I reiterated, "No! Identify and manage your manager."

They both laughed.

"How to identify your manager?" Anuj wondered.

I said, "You will understand when I explain it in detail. It's already time to go, so let's meet at the same time tomorrow in Kamatibaug."

They agreed.

Who is your manager?

WE OURSELVES ACT AS OUR OWN MANAGERS
TEA
NANJA

orning walk is best in Kamatibaug, the largest community garden in Baroda. I heard that when King Sayajirao Gaekwad III, (11 March 1863 – 6 February 1939), the most famous monarch of Baroda, decided to build a large garden for the people of his state, he formed a committee in charge of designing the garden. Once the garden was finished, the committee named it Sayajibaug after their great king Sayajirao Gaekwad. However, the people of Baroda called it Kamatibaug (*Kamati* means Committee and *baug* means garden in the local language). I researched a little to find out the authenticity of this story and discovered it to be an asset to Baroda City. Every morning, hundreds of people come to this garden to walk, jog, meditate, bike, or just sit and chat. I had completed my two rounds of running around the garden before I got Anuj's call. He was standing next to the birds' section of the zoo. I asked him to wait, and then I continued my run.

Anuj and Siddharth were gazing at the Butterfly Park, which was still under construction. Siddharth immediately said, "These people are ready to spoil this place. Why are they creating another concrete structure within the garden? It will destroy the garden."

I asked, "Do you know what was here before this construction started?"

"They must have cut some trees to build it," he replied confidently.

"Most of our opinions are based on perceptions. We think that people in the government are evil, so they can only do bad stuff. If something good is being built, something bad must have happened. If no tree was cut, some people must have taken bribes," I retorted.

"But tell me whether it is true or not. These people don't receive enough salaries as we do, so they take bribes to meet their needs," Siddharth said with self-assurance.

I just informed him of all the facts, and he was both surprised and happy to know about the Butterfly Park coming into existence there. He realized that some hardworking people had made this decision to further beautify the city, and this park was being built out of sheer dedication and hard work. No other motive was behind it.

We left the garden and sat on a bench next to a famous tea shop. During Vadfest (Vadodara Festival), this place was decorated, with lots of areas to sit and chat.

"This world operates based on perceptions. Few obvious facts build people's understanding, and they lack the time to find out the entire body of facts. Negative perception grows easily and faster," I said.

"Yes!" They both agreed, but I could sense their curiosity about what I meant exactly by "how to identify and manage your manager." Siddharth started asking about it, and I was happy to take that thread of conversation.

"Anybody who manages the work assigned to you and your team ensures that he or she obtains the best outcome. You know how the whole process works. The manager also evaluates your performance to tell you how you have done your work. You are the one who does the work, but you always need somebody external to review and evaluate how well you have done the job. Based on the staff performance and the budget allocated, the manager decides on salary raises or job designations," I said.

After a moment, I continued, "Nonetheless, the reality is that we ourselves act as our own managers through our self-directed work performance. There should be no reason for us to care about impressing our managers specifically."

Anuj said impatiently, "The managers are the ones who decide our salary increases and promotions, so they are powerful, aren't they?"

"Do you think that your manager decides your salary increase and promotion?" I paused. "You need to perform well and to satisfy certain criteria to be promoted or to receive a raise, don't you?

"You're the one who decides your salary increase and promotion. But in your perception, your fear that your manager won't grant your deserved promotion or raise is a major factor. The *manager* that you have been talking about for two days now is that fear. No individual creates that fear within you; you are the one who sets up and maintains it.

"If your manager recognizes your inner fear, he manipulates it. Once your fear is exposed, you have no way to satisfy your manager. That is the time when you have to depend on either luck or lick.

"On the other hand, if your manager is an effective leader and recognizes the fear within you, he will certainly help you overcome it. But a good leader would also expect you to treat your colleagues respectfully, so give your best performance even if your manager is not around. It means that your life will be tougher if you think about satisfying your manager because you have to strive to get along with your co-workers although it is not possible to please everybody." I stopped for breath.

We had finished our tea, and it was getting hotter by now. "Are you trying to say that there is no way out? We have to keep pleasing people to succeed. In that case, I will have to leave this profession. I cannot do things to satisfy others," Siddharth said.

"How serious are you, Siddharth? Can you leave your job today?" I asked.

"Not today. I have to find a new job, and then I will resign. I am not searching just yet because I still have some hope left with this company."

"What if you are fired today?" I challenged Siddharth.

"Ohh! Don't say such scary stuff early in the morning, Sakti. I just bought a house on loan and still repaying back to bank. My aging father is not well. My brother does not have a job yet. I will be terribly affected. I can't think of such things."

Siddharth's voice sounded small and thoughtful. Complete silence followed.

"That's our manager. Fear! We don't dare to talk about it. You work to stay away from your fear. You push your fear further but can never get rid of it. The only way that you think you can keep fear away from you is money, so you want more of it. When the person who decides on the amount of money you should receive becomes your only source of hope and fear, that's your manager," I said.

"But it's not always about money and salary increase. It's also about the work distribution, recognition, sense of self-worth within the team, and so on. They also play significant roles. I may get real money, but if my team or manager does not treat me respectfully, then I would not feel happy. That's not fear but..." Anuj stopped, trying to find an appropriate word.

"Self-respect," Siddharth completed Anuj's statement.

"Who determines whether you should earn respect and recognition? Your manager?" I asked.

"Yes, we do our jobs, but he is the one who decides our status in the organization. If he respects me, my fellow team members will do the same," Siddharth explained.

"Hmmm... Shall we meet again tomorrow, which happens to be a Saturday? At Pavilion Ground at 6:00 a.m. Meantime, think about Shiva's business, perception, and who gives recognition," I concluded.

"Sure," they said together and left.

It was 7:30 a.m. The sun had come out of its early kindness and was making it tougher for anyone to sit outside any longer.

Smart employee: are you one?

PLAYING EXPERIENCE WERE BEAUTIFUL
IN OUR TEAM THERE ARE NO BEAUTIFUL FACES...
HAHA.
NANDA

Running on Pavilion Ground makes one feel like a sports person. Kids from different schools and colleges playing different games and doing different exercises make a person feel happy. Vadodara (Baroda) is a city of and for the youth. People see youthfulness in every corner of the city. Whether it's food, sports, art, culture, festivities, studies, or romance, Vadodara youths immerse in all of these with fun and conviction. Definitely, Maharaja Sayajirao University plays a significant role. One football flew near me, and I ran to kick it. It gave me great pleasure to do so after so many years. By the time I completed one round of running, I found Anuj and Siddharth already in our meeting place. They were watching the young ladies playing basketball but quickly shifted their attention as soon as they saw me.

"Let's play basketball," I said.

They were both ready, and we went to the basketball court. I asked the girls, "Can we play with you?"

After a few giggles from several of the five-member team, one said, "Sure."

We started playing. I was a miserable player, but Anuj and Siddharth were doing their best. The girls were losing badly. However, after a few minutes, Anuj and Siddharth got tired; the girls took control and won. This was because the girls had been playing for a long time, while the two software engineers were mostly sleeping or working for the past several years.

We thanked the girls for allowing us to play. We then sat on a bench.

"How do you like the morning so far?" I asked.

"The best morning so far. Starting tomorrow, we will come here every day to play. Great exercise," Anuj said.

"But are you not disappointed that you lost?" I prodded.

"Naah! The company and the playing experience were beautiful. I enjoyed every bit of it," Anuj replied.

"But nobody cheered for you. Those girls might be thinking that you guys are losers," I teased them.

Siddharth understood which direction I was going. He said, "Yes, respect and recognition didn't matter here because we enjoyed every bit of it. If we play and lose every day, we may not come here again. This is what happens at work. We enjoy working with our new team, company, or manager for the first few days, but after that, we need some other reason to motivate us."

"What if you play every day and win on some days and lose on others? Will you still stop?" I asked.

"No. With such company, never!" Anuj said with a big smile on his face.

"But unfortunately in our team, there are no beautiful faces." Siddharth said and they both laughed.

"I understand! It's the people who matter a lot, but the image you create for yourself plays a significant role in how others treat you. Others look beautiful or horrifying, depending on how they treat you. It means that people around you will look nice if you create a good self-image in front of them. If your team likes you, then your manager ought to like you because he or she is also driven by the fear of losing a good employee whom everybody likes. If the manager upsets this kind of people, then he or she will upset the team. A manager will never dare to do that. Recognition and respect follow the team spirit. No need to make any extra effort to earn respect or recognition," I said.

"But it's not easy to make everybody happy in the team," Anuj protested.

"I also do not like to make people—who don't deserve to be part of the team—happy," Siddharth said.

"I never said, 'Please others.' I said, 'Create a good self-image and maintain it,'" I clarified.

"Today I will take an hour to explain six different areas we must focus on so that we become not only good but also smart employees. Smart employees are those who do not only manage their careers but also effectively handle their managers," I said.

"Shall we have some breakfast while learning this lesson? I am very hungry now," Anuj said.

"Good idea! Let's go to Madras Café near the bus stop. They serve nice South Indian food," Siddharth added.

We all walked from Pavilion Ground to Madras Café.

Feed the food chain

Madras cafe
WHO IS THE MANAGER?
IN REAL TERMS, NOBODY IS...
MYSORE MASALA DOSA...
NANDA

adras Café is a traditional South Indian restaurant that aims to serve people who travel by bus or train. It is easy to come here and grab a snack or a meal just before catching a long-distance bus or train. Usually, people don't spend a lot of time in this restaurant; thus, they focus more on the quality of the food than on comfort. As far as taste is concerned, this is one of the best South Indian restaurants in the city.

Despite the setup and the owner's expectation that people who come here would leave as soon as they finish their meals, we chose to spend a couple of hours there to take the discussion further.

I asked Anuj and Siddharth to tell me who this restaurant's manager was.

At first, both turned their heads toward the cashier who was sitting just next to the entrance. Unlike the case in sophisticated restaurants, the server gives you a handwritten bill when you indicate that you don't want anything more. Then you have to take the bill to the cashier and pay before leaving the restaurant.

While the search for the manager was still on, one of the servers came, placed three glasses of water and a jug on our table, and looked at us, expecting our order. Anuj and Siddharth shifted their focus from the cashier to the server, wondering whether this guy was the manager. Observing our blank looks, the server went away, assuming that we had not yet decided what we wanted to eat. He started taking an order from another table.

"So, who is the manager?" I asked again.

"In real terms, nobody is. All are showing equal ownership, and they respect one another," Siddharth said.

Meantime, Anuj was trying to call the server's attention to order food, but the server was so busy that he did not notice

Anuj's hand gestures. The cashier observed this for a few seconds and then approached us to take our order. Anuj ordered three *Mysore masala dosa* (Popular South Indian breakfast) and looked at us. We nodded to confirm our agreement with his choice. Then the cashier went to the server, gave him our order, and went back to his work station. The server walked up to the kitchen, shouting, "Three *Mysore masala dosa!*" The cook did not give any indication of acknowledgment but went to the hot pan and poured three cups of batter on three spots of a big pan, which was already hot.

"These guys work like links on a chain. Each of them is connected with the others; thus, no single person runs this show. The business runs, depending on how well they coordinate with one another. I would say that the customer is the main driver here. Customers will keep going to this place as long as the restaurant people serve good food, and they will be able to do so only if they work together," Anuj said.

"Excellent! Now let's think from the organization's perspective," I began.

"We are all part of a food chain. Your performance helps your manager make a good impression, his own performance helps his manager, and so on. When the entire chain performs well, then the organization performs well, resulting in its financial success. Stockholders invest in the organization when they see a predictable return on investment. More investment in the company means more benefits for its employees, increased job security, and more freedom to perform their duties.

"Now, when we do not do a good job, this chain weakens or breaks up. For an employee, it might be just one instance where he or she fails to do a good job, but your entire chain becomes affected. Your manager values you when you feed the food chain by outperforming on every occasion. Your performance beyond expectations helps your manager make a good impression on his manager up the chain. To ensure you are feeding the food chain, focus on key areas, which I will now discuss.

Perform like never before

"The first key area is to perform like never before. We have to constantly reinvent ourselves to remain relevant in this complex and competitive world. Your performance and achievements of yesterday belong to the past, and there is no point in finding opportunities to cash them. Efforts to perform every time with a newbie mentality are more worthy than wasting time explaining to others how good you were in your previous team, company, or with your former manager. By newbie mentality, I mean *zero baggage* of achievements. It is similar to the case of a door-to-door salesperson. The door-to-door salesperson cannot come to my house and tell me that because my neighbor purchased the item that he or she is selling, I should buy it as well. He or she has to start from the beginning every time. We are all door-to-door salespeople, and every day, we face a new door. So start anew every day, and perform as never before.

Help the manager with weak areas

"The second key area is to help the manager with weak areas. To successfully manage your manager, you must understand their limitations, and help address those limitations, without them feeling self-conscious about it, best employees make their manager's life easier by helping them overcome their weaknesses and they do it for their manager seamlessly with minimal direction and hassle.

"Leaders from the human resources world advice employees to 'Find out what keeps your boss up at night.' Whatever those issues, projects, or roadblocks are, have an honest conversation about them, and offer to pitch in.

"In this entire process, avoid making either your manager or anybody in the organization feel that you are consciously doing it because you know your manager's weak areas. It can hurt your manager's ego. I suggest that first, identify those areas. Next, start investing time and effort in those areas as if you are ensuring that your entire team is being helped.

"Be sincere by telling your manager, 'I feel that as a team, we need to focus more on these areas; therefore, I am putting more effort into them.' Now it will not look like your manager's weakness but the whole team's. This way, you will give less hints to anybody that you are doing these to cover your manager." I paused.

"My manager is horrible at passing tough messages clearly. He always avoids situations like those. Last night, he wanted to communicate that we had to stay late and finish the work although it came later in the afternoon. He was so uncomfortable that it was visible. When I was packing my bag to go home, he asked me whether I could stay to finish the work. I immediately agreed, but his facial expression was really funny. Sometimes, he does the work himself instead of telling anybody to do so," Siddharth said.

"So, what could you have done there?" I asked.

"I could have told him to hold a quick staff meeting and request everybody to stay, and then I could stay with them, which I did," Siddharth replied.

"What would you have done, considering the point I mentioned just now?" I asked Anuj.

"I would have called for a quick meeting of the whole team and informed them that we had to finish the work that night because..." Anuj stopped in mid-sentence.

"You don't know the reason why you have to stay, so it's difficult to convince others. Right?" I prodded.

"I can ask my manager why he is asking me to stay late. I did so last night. It was because the testers in the US would have to test and certify the software on the same day. The client was threatening to leave us if we did not deliver it by the end of the day, US time," Siddharth said.

"Excellent! Now, Anuj, continue," I prompted him.

"Friends, we have a situation. Our client is upset because without the fix that we are currently working on, it is blocking their ability to use the system. Shall we stay as a team, finish it tonight, and deliver it to our testers in the US so that it can be delivered to our client by the end of business day over there?" Anuj said with great conviction.

"Excellent! Good job, Anuj. Any problem doing it?" I asked.

"No problem as such, but if I do it often, don't you think that my manager will think that I'm trying to take over his role?" Siddharth asked.

"He may. Ask your manager's permission before doing so. This way, he will be relieved that you are covering the area that he is not good at. He will also get the impression that you are not thinking that you are greater than him. In many situations, managers will encourage such behavior," I explained.

The server brought the food. The moment food was kept on the table, Siddharth started eating. He didn't even bother to look at us till he finished half of his *dosa*. We could clearly make it that he was terribly hungry.

We both were looking at him eating. He looked at us and was embarrassed.

"I can't stop eating when I see food in front me of me. You can get anything done by me by promising me food," Siddharth justified. We both started laughing and he joined us.

"Some things just drive us without we putting any effort. Like food for Siddharth. You may call it motivator," I continued.

Identify your manager's motivation

"The next key area is to identify your manager's motivation. What he or she considers the most important. If he or she is a detail-oriented person, then talk to him or her about the finer points. If he or she is a visionary, then provide the big picture and so on.

"Understanding why your manager does or cares about certain things can give you insights into his or her management style. Sometimes we assume a lot more than the reality. Similar to every human being, your manager gets motivated by or cares about certain factors; thus, he or she behaves in a particular way.

"Understanding your manager's value system requires careful observation and time. To expedite this matter, simply ask your manager what he or she cares about the most. Sometimes it is difficult to get it out at the first meeting, but with constant observation and continuous efforts, this goal can be achieved in a couple of interactions. Make your intentions clear to your manager because it might arouse his or her curiosity about what's cooking," I explained.

Make every follow-up an opportunity for improvement

"My manager is irritating at times. He keeps following up every now and then. This makes me feel that he thinks I'm an idiot," Siddharth said.

"Good point, but do you know the reason?" I asked.

"I feel that he just panics. Don't know how he became a manager," Siddharth responded immediately.

Smiling at his all-too-common analysis, I explained, "The next key area is to make every follow-up an opportunity for improvement. Every time you are asked about the status of a particular project or task that you are working on is an opportunity for improvement. If your manager is inquiring about your current task, it indicates that you have raised a question in his mind about you or your task. There may be many reasons for the question, but you have to understand every reason and address it to avoid repeat follow-ups.

"Your manager wants to know the status, either for a report to somebody higher up or for his own information. This situation also indicates that either you have not provided him the status proactively, or no formal tool or mechanism does so on a regular basis. For whatever reason, the onus is on you to fix the status-reporting issue. Not knowing the status of your project or task makes your manager uncomfortable, and every occasion of discomfort or every question mark will damage the food chain.

"Another reason is that he may not be confident about your performance and wants to ensure that you don't cause him trouble by giving him unpleasant news just when he is expecting task completion. This is a serious problem. This doubt in your manager's mind means that you are way below the mark at which he is expecting you to perform.

"One more reason for your manager's follow-up is when he wants to initiate a conversation but isn't sure where to start. So it is easy to begin with the project or task that you are working on.

"It becomes difficult to identify the actual reason for your manager's follow-up. Hence, the first step is to ensure that you proactively communicate the status of the project or task on a regular basis and in a predictable manner. If you are still being asked about the status, then it's time for an open discussion. Tell him how you feel about his seeming lack of confidence in your performance. Seek the steps that you can take to help him develop confidence in your ability. This conversation can be tough to start, but once you open up, you will see wonders."

Siddharth and Anuj were listening attentively. I continued.

Know what your manager needs

"Another important key area is to know what your manager needs. Many times, managers expect people to be mind readers, simply because they're busy and can't always go over all the details of a project. As such, your manager might forget to tell you some information, such as a firm deadline or a required step. Since everyone operates from his or her set of realities, the possibility of miscommunication is high. That's why you need to take the initiative to set expectations for every project that your manager assigns to you. Do you need to find out: 'What is the deadline? What are my resources? What checkpoints or milestones do we want to establish, if any? What step or contact person is critical to this project?'"

"When you're dealing with a micromanager, head off his or her requests by anticipating them and getting things done before they come to you. You may not do it right when you start working with a micromanager. Once you realize that your manager is telling you how to do your job now and then, it means he or she is micromanaging. From that moment, observe your manager carefully. Start involving him or her in every matter, and share your plans on how to do it. It may take a couple of weeks to a couple of months, but the time will come when your manager will show disinterest in your updates and let you do your job your way. This will indicate that you have won the confidence of your super-critical manager.

"Just as you set expectations when dealing with clients and co-workers, you need to manage your relationship with your boss and set expectations every time."

"What if my manager, despite all my efforts, is unsatisfied with my work? What if others, such as my manager's manager or his counterparts, decide what good work should be?" Anuj asked. He was hesitating to disclose much information about his manager, whom he knew was my good friend.

Find out what's *good* and who decides it

I responded, "Good point, Anuj. This brings up another key area to find out what's good and who decides it. Whether you report to one or four managers, make sure you're meeting everyone's expectations. After all, what seems good to you may be mediocre to your manager or his boss or counterpart. Therefore, find out what is good to each manager to whom you report. You could only ask him or her, 'How is good determined in this project? If this proceeded exactly as you wanted and turned out perfect, what would have to happen between now and that time?' As an added benefit, you might even get an idea of the full scope of the project. Sometimes managers don't tell you much, and you have to pull it out of them. If you do this simple step upfront and find out what the expectations are on the project and the timelines, you save a lot of time in the end."

"These are well-intentioned bosses whom you are talking about. I have worked for some unethical ones. They would tell me to do something, and when I do, they would wash their hands of it, especially when it goes wrong. Others even make good comments about everything during the year, but in the appraisal, they write bad evaluations that they never said throughout the year," Siddharth said.

Document everything

"Good point, Siddharth. Yes, some bosses are like that. So I would suggest documenting your interactions with your manager—whether requests or criticisms—so you can refer to them when needed. This is another key area which I wanted to bring up here. That is, document everything.

"Technology can help in documenting. Many free tools are available in the market, where you can track tasks and feedback, and keep your manager informed. This way, neither you nor your manager will forget the tasks.

"When your manager asks you for something, put it in writing. Create an email trail of all requests, as well as everything you produce. If your manager is the type who gives you verbal directions, follow up with an email that outlines the discussion to ensure that you heard everything correctly. Cover yourself at all times, and be prepared to pull out your documented proof if your manager questions your outputs. I understand that it entails extra effort, but it comes handy when you have to explain a situation," I pointed out.

Two servings of breakfast were over. We had delicious *dosa* and then *vada* (Popular Indian savory snacks). Since we had occupied a table longer than expected, we could see the server and the cashier giving us a questioning look. So we decided to leave but were not sure where to go.

Siddharth suggested driving to the Mahi River bank. That was a quiet place where we could spend the rest of the day. None of us had any other engagement, making it a perfect day to enjoy with friends.

Focus on flow

IF YOU ARE MAKING MISTAKES, IT MEANS YOU ARE GROWING...

Once we settled on a nice spot near the river, Anuj looked at me. I was about to ask them the same question, when Anuj joked, "Now don't tell me who the manager is here." We all laughed.

"What is the name of this river Siddharth?" I asked.

"I never came here. I thought I knew all about Vadodara. Is there any significance of this river?" Anuj extended my question further.

Siddharth said, "Mahi is considered an auspicious river. Its full name is Mahisagar. It is one of the rivers that flow from east to west in our country. Vadodara City was built on the river banks of Mahi River."

I was deep in thought when Anuj suggested, "Let's continue our discussion."

"Do you see the river flowing? Isn't it as effortless as breathing?" I commented.

"I would say that the river manages its surroundings without giving a single instruction. It is mighty but offers a soothing experience. It serves yet leads. It is truly a servant leader. Our managers should be like rivers," Siddharth reflected.

Taking his lead, I responded, "I agree! No dispute there. The river also reminds me of another key aspect that will make us successful in any situation, irrespective of any manager and at any stage of our careers or lives. It is effortless communication flow.

"Communication is the key ingredient of success. Communication can be compared to salt in food. Your technical skills, ability to perform your job functions, behavior, and attitude are essential to your success, but if communication, the main ingredient, is missing, then you will require lots of time to prove yourself.

"Your ability to communicate your work, thought, objective, intention, and vision determines your ability to feed the food chain. Out of all aspects of communication, I suggest focusing on effectively conveying your intention behind any action you take and the result you want. Your manager may have a different way of getting things done, and your suggested new idea may be rejected if you do not clearly express your purpose and expected outcome.

"Communication has to go both ways for success. If your manager upsets you or misunderstands you, speak up, not from the head, but from the heart. One way to do so is with an 'I' message. For example, 'I was upset and hurt by what you said. I interpreted it as ___________. Did you mean it that way?' Most people want to be heard, yet many don't get heard by their managers. Therefore, it's your responsibility to talk when you're not feeling heard. If you're reluctant to speak to your boss, first try this approach on your family members. Practice it in a safe environment before trying it on your boss.

Be proactive with communication

"If you are making mistakes, it means you are growing. Everybody makes mistakes; if anybody does not, then he or she has not started anything new. But mistakes are also the reasons why we lose our managers' confidence. Hence, it is essential to learn from a mistake and erase the bitter taste in everybody's mouth about this fault. The only effective way to achieve both is by admitting your mistake to your manager, with greater emphasis on learning from the error. Learning from the blunder should be genuine, and you must admit it with all honesty. The timing of admitting a mistake is also extremely essential. Do it as soon as possible and in a written format to ensure that you can state your points in an organized way and that it is correctly interpreted. Filters in listening are much more than in reading."

"I do not understand this part," Siddharth interrupted.

"Let me explain from one of my life incidents. In the early days of my career, my manager trusted me with a complex client issue and asked me to make the necessary changes to the client's live environment to fix the problem. I did not ask lots of questions as I thought I knew everything about it. But after completing my task, I realized that I completely messed up the client system. I resolved the problem, but due to a mistake, it would impact the client the next time when they would try to perform the same activity one month later.

"My manager had left for home by then. I called him and explained the situation. He had to return to the office, and after reviewing the matter, he realized that we had to fix a lot of things, which might take hours. It was already 10:00 p.m. He called his wife to tell her that he would come home very late and informed me that I could leave. I insisted on staying and fixing it myself. We both worked for two hours more and fixed the entire situation. I apologized and clearly explained what I did wrong and how I could avoid it next time. He was very understanding and appreciated my telling the truth promptly and sharing what I learned from the mistake. He trusted me more than ever from that day onward.

"Everybody is insecure in this fast-changing world. If you have the right state of mind and communicate the real state of a situation, then you help your manager understand the situation better, provide some relief, and would thus be more trustworthy.

Go beyond the call of duty

"Siddharth rightly pointed out why the river could be called a servant leader. We must all play the role of a leader and specifically, a servant leader, to help both the community and ourselves. You cannot expect extraordinary results by doing only what's expected. You are paid for what you are expected to do. You still have your job because you give value for the money that you are receiving as a salary. Do not expect anything extra for doing your duty. Hence, if you desire to strengthen your position where your value will increase, then you have to go beyond the call of duty.

"Once you finish your tasks, it's your duty to search and find out who needs help. How can you help remove a roadblock from the path of your project's success? If somebody is slow, then approach him and offer your help in completing his work. If you know that a team member makes mistakes, then review her work to help her find the mistakes ahead of time. But it is important to ensure that you make your intentions clear and ask their permission before doing anything."

"This is impossible. We are in a competitive world. If I help others complete their work, then how will I have the advantage of staying ahead of them? They are very smart. They will not tell anybody that I helped them and will take full credit. You don't know my teammates," Anuj protested.

Help your competitor

"That's the catch. Your competitor wins when you lose temporarily. But you win permanently when you make your competitor win. In the professional world, individual wins are temporary successes. It might give you personal satisfaction but would create more dissatisfaction in your team due to their inability to succeed as well. It is essential to understand the big picture and not focus solely on your individual success but on how to help your competitors succeed so that your entire team succeeds. Moreover, you must ensure that you do not publish any evidence that you have assisted your competitor. This will create fondness for you within the team. It will take the distrust out of the competitor's mind about your intention. This will help you win over the long term, irrespective of who wins at first. This team culture makes it a winning team, making your food chain the strongest," I explained.

"I still don't agree with this. Philosophically, it might sound right, but practically, it wouldn't work," Anuj argued.

"Have you tried it?" I asked.

"Yes."

"How long?"

"Not long enough, but my colleagues rejected me. They assumed that I wanted to show off to the manager that I was more intelligent and thus helping them."

"Was that thought unnatural?"

"No," he admitted.

"It is understandable for people to feel that way. Don't expect any positive response immediately. Just keep the serving mentality in mind and try assisting others in whatever way you can. Just like this river. Don't people throw garbage into it? But does the river stop flowing because of that? That's the reason why rivers are revered in Bharat. The point is if you turn yourself into a great human being by serving others, you will be revered by others in due time, and that includes your manager.

"It takes time and sincerity. People will throw garbage at you and question your intention, but if your goal is long-term growth, then that's the right way," I concluded.

Anuj was not satisfied but understood.

Free yourself

MONEY..?
LEARNING IS AN ONGOING PROCESS...
NANDA

Siddharth plucked a grass blade from the ground and asked, "So you mean to say, we should become saints so that everybody starts respecting us, including our managers, and that's the way we can manage our managers?" I could detect satire in his voice.

"Good point, Siddharth. It seems you are not convinced of the fact that you should help your competitor. Fair enough! Let's examine ourselves first. Why are we working?" I asked.

"For money," Anuj and Siddharth both responded at once.

"Money, meaning...?" I probed further.

Anuj took out his wallet and showed cash. We all laughed.

"That's just part of your income," I said.

"You mean career growth and so on?" Siddharth countered.

I started explaining, "We are all working for three major incomes. The first is salary, which will give us enough money to live our desired lifestyles. The second is learning by working on a project or being part of a team, which has a constant reason for learning new stuff every day. The third is the work environment, where you feel you are important. I call these the three types of currencies that we expect to earn from our day jobs. We must keep account of these three currencies."

"I can understand money and learning, but the work environment does not represent earnings," Siddharth argued.

"Let me ask you a question. Who is the best team member in your team, excluding you?" I asked.

"Rishabh," Siddharth responded immediately.

"Why?"

"He is knowledgeable, predictable, and my good friend. He is the sole guy on my team whom I like working with. No ego, no competition."

"So that third factor—your friend—makes him the chosen one beyond his ability to deliver work and his knowledge, right?" I asked.

"I call that the work environment or energy currency," I clarified further. "We all know that in our day jobs, we are expected to deliver more than what we earn. Hence, I would like to explain these three factors from a different perspective.

Earnings

"My salary, stocks, and perks are the earnings for the functions I am expected to perform at work. How would I know if I am delivering the results as expected? Most of the time, I translate the outcome into the performance rating I receive during appraisal and the feedback from my manager. To stay valuable, I have to deliver more than is expected from me.

"Does my manager, supervisor, leader, or anybody to whom I am accountable for my work have to follow up to know its status?

"Do I create a 'wow feeling' for the work I deliver?

"Am I available for more work if my supervisor or manager wants something done?

"Am I predictable in my deliveries with respect to time and quality?

"Does my manager find a rescuing friend in me when he or she needs any help?

"If I answer 'yes' to all of these, then my manager values me more than the salary paid to me.

Education/learning

"I am expected to possess the knowledge and skill required for a project. It may be technical expertise, functional/product/domain knowledge, or process knowledge. But focusing on a particular area and developing expertise in it will make you valuable to the team.

"Learning is an ongoing process, so it must continue. Over a certain period, you are expected to acquire expertise in many such areas, which will keep you relevant and valuable. But the software engineering field is a tough area for remaining valuable because others in the team will reach your level at some point in time, and you will soon be replaced. So an important factor is to ensure how you create your brand and remain valuable at a global level, beyond just within the team.

"In today's world, going global is not difficult. You can have a blog site, contribute to digital forums on a regular basis, and present papers at different conferences to continue maintaining your relevance in the global arena, as well as help you remain valuable in your team or company.

Environment

"This area requires soft skills. If your presence makes your team feel comfortable, enjoyable, and safe, then you are a valuable member. You will always face challenges in maintaining this status due to competition, selfish motives of some individuals, and grudge/jealousy towards you due to your growth or importance.

"This area requires your constant attention, and you must remain alert all the time to make sure you don't make others feel uncomfortable.

"While the most used technique is to showcase what you have achieved so that others recognize that you are valuable, that can easily turn into a reason for discomfort within the team. It is essential to first have self-confidence that you are good in what you do, and people like your presence. Once you train your brain to believe it, you can work toward helping your fellow team members, colleagues, and manager so that they succeed as well.

"This selfless effort sometimes does not give the desired results within a short duration because your competitors feel that you are doing this to grab attention and suspect ulterior motives behind your actions. But have patience and keep doing this selfless act till your fellow team members realize that you are not merely acting but are sincerely nice to them.

"Once you feel good about being in tune with the team, do not stop there, but start contributing to organizational-level undertakings, such as cultural events, sports, and community service. Your contributions to the team make you valuable to the team, but your contributions to the organization make you valuable to the organization, thus expanding your presence in the organization.

"If you do all these steps and have enough currency in your bank, then you are free from the fear of losing your job because you will have many opportunities to choose from.

"Once you have all these advantages, you are not only making yourself more valuable to the organization, but you are also making yourself more marketable. If you are consciously working toward these goals for a longer period, you can see a sea of opportunities coming to you. You will have more than one option to choose from, within the organization, as well as in our industry."

"I guess I am good at all these but unsure because I never thought of it this way," Anuj said.

I responded, "I suggest maintaining and regularly updating a document that reflects all the good work you are doing to increase your value. That document can be your résumé."

"You mean CV. I have that ready, but it only lists all my certifications and education details, along with work experience," Anuj said.

"Good. Keep your résumé up to date. I would rather suggest creating a future résumé that states all accomplishments you would like to see in your profile at the next level. This should be no more than a single page. Once you create the résumé, highlight the areas where you are not there yet. Focus on those areas to ensure your growth toward the goals you have set.

"The only challenge in the résumé is that it lists all the projects and education that you have completed but cannot justify your soft skills or your soft contributions to the team. In this case, professional networking sites play a major role. Write articles and participate in discussions about these soft skills to share thoughts and ideas about building a great team. Current recruiters review your social profile even before calling you for an interview, so your contributions in these forums fill the gap that a résumé cannot," I explained.

"But what if your manager doesn't care and never looks at your accomplishments. I went to my manager twice, asking when I could be promoted. He said all sorts of stories but has never promoted me. I will not leave him until he promotes me," Siddharth said.

Free your manager

GO AGAINST YOU?
BE A PROBLEM SOLVER...
TUNE YOUR INSTRUMENT...
NANDA

"""D""o you think that your pressure will help you get a promotion?" I asked.

"Not putting pressure will not help either," he responded.

"We always look up to our managers for our promotions, salary increases, and better projects. This is not bad, but sometimes unknowingly, we put pressure on our managers, which discomforts them due to their inability to give what we ask." I said

"It is important to convey what you expect and to do so at the right time. Expressing your desire for a promotion or a salary increase just before the appraisal does not give enough room for the manager to work toward it; sometimes, you receive lame excuses. Ensure that you inform the manager long before the appraisal time or in the beginning of the period covered by the appraisal, and seek the activities or tasks that you must be doing to achieve them.

"Once you ask and receive the details of the expectations, do not mention any promotion or salary increase; just focus on those tasks. Giving a regular update on your progress will help the manager keep working toward your desire." I paused.

"You mean to say not to ask for promotion once we know what all tasks we need to do in order to get promotion. But what if he forgets about the promotion." Anuj asked.

"Promotions are earned by your efforts. It is always a better state to remain slightly under recognized than over recognized. If you deserve promotion, then nobody can stop getting you. It may get delayed but it should be your manager's worry. Getting promotion before others feel you are due puts you in a risky spot and may be detrimental to your career. If you seek promotion too often and put pressure on your manager it may go against you," I explained.

"What do you mean by go against you?" Siddharth asked.

"If you desire something impossible or difficult to get in the current organization or at that moment, then it may work against you. The manager will assume that you are looking for something that this organization cannot give and will thus try to train your replacement and not pay a lot of attention to your desire. So be very careful about what you ask. A detailed study on what can be achieved and a discussion with your manager about how to plan your career rather than what you want will avoid your being pushed to a corner.

"While it is important to share what you expect, understand your manager's compulsions to avoid putting him or her on the spot if your request is not granted. This gives a comforting feeling to your manager. Hence, he or she will work toward your desired goal in his or her way rather than being forced to work per your terms.

"We put other pressures on our managers, expecting that they know everything. Understand that your manager is a co-employee with abilities and disabilities. Rather than always expecting him or her to be more intelligent than you, try to give options other than asking for a decision to be made. Your manager may not take any of your options but come up with a new alternative as a solution, but your proposals for a resolution will remove the pressure from your manager to think afresh and indicate that you do a thorough job of every task given to you.

"You may at times have suggestions for some areas that are not under your influence. In that case, giving options will make your manager feel that you are trying to take control over the aspects under his or her own authority. This approach may work against you. Hence, it is important that when you are crossing the boundary, ask an open-ended question that might drive him or her to answer what you want.

"Be a problem solver, not a problem creator. Problems will always be with us, but sometimes, the easiest way to resolve an issue is first to stop participating in it. A good problem solver doesn't create drama or add to the crisis. Never bring a problem to your boss without at least one good strategy for dealing with it. At the heart of great leadership and successful management is being the best problem solver you can be.

"Stay calm even when everything around you is in a state of chaos. When everything is falling apart and breaking down, the last thing you want is losing your cool. It is easy to be great when matters are calm, but if you truly want to stand out, the smart approach is learning to be calm in chaos. When everybody else is losing their temper or showing irritation, the smartest way is a level-headed and reasonable reaction.

"Don't blame others, but always hold yourself accountable. Your life, business, and reputation are all that you make them to be. Don't blame others if you mess up or fail. Instead, take responsibility with a summary of what you did wrong, what can be done to make it better, and how you will prevent it from happening again. Accountability is increasingly rare, making it even more valuable."

"It seems like I have to manage myself to succeed, and my manager is instrumental in my career growth but is just one among many," Siddharth said.

"Absolutely! If you define your manager as your fear, aspiration, motivation, and interpersonal skills, then that's all you have to manage. Your real manager is just one instrument to help you get ahead in your career," I explained.

"But the problem is that instrument. If he or she is not paying close attention, then all my efforts will go waste," Siddharth said.

"I agree! So ensure that you tune your instrument appropriately and promptly."

Tune your instrument

I THINK THEY ENJOY THEIR LIFE THE MOST...

"Do you know what's the most painful process for a manager," I asked.

"Oh! Painful process, for manager? I think they enjoy their life the most. All pain is for us, they just gain," Siddharth said.

"I would not agree with Siddharth. I think choosing whom to promote among many and how much salary to give whom must be very difficult," Anuj said.

I responded, "Let me explain the appraisal process for you. During the appraisal period, all managers go through an exercise called stack ranking. This is the way to rate all employees in a sequential order. The top-rated employees are slated to receive the best out of the ratings, promotions, and salaries. Stack ranking is a painful process for any manager because it is extremely difficult to rate two employees of similar caliber. If you can make it easier for your manager, then you have higher chances of being at the top of the stack rank. For this, I suggest an easy technique."

"Oh Really! So there is a technique to get promoted. Please continue I am listening," Siddharth said

I started explaining, "Ask your manager to rate you on a scale of 1 to 10 in the beginning of the appraisal period, which is mostly at the start of the calendar year. On the scale, 10 means you are the top employee in his or her team, and 1 means you are at the bottom. When you first throw this question, and if you are not the best or the worst, your manager will likely give you a 5 rating. Irrespective of your manager's rating, take note of it without asking for the reason behind the score. Next, ask what you can do to advance to the next level, for example, from 5 to 6. Your manager will give you some suggestions. Take note of these and ask clarifying questions until you are clear on what you must do."

"Now it's time to act. Do the recommended actions consistently till you meet the next time. Ask the same question after providing the status of what you did about those tasks. Continue working until you reach the next higher point. Once you do, ask again for the actions you must take to progress to the next level. Continue this exercise till you achieve a rating of 9 or 10.

"If your manager can tell you confidently that you are one of his or her top employees, then you must ask what you can do to retain that spot.

"Regular one-on-one meetings are the occasions when you must do this activity. If your manager does not schedule a regular one-on-one, do so with his or her permission. This will not only show how serious you are about your performance but also feed your manager's mind with the thought about what he or she can do for your further development.

"In some organizations, managers are not accessible due to various reasons. In that case, find an alternative mechanism to get your answers. Knowing your performance level is your right, so do not shy away from asking this question."

"What if my manager never shows up? Our lead is the main person here. He makes the decisions," Anuj said.

"Do you meet regularly with your lead?" I asked.

"Yes. We have weekly one-on-one meetings. I do meet with my manager once every two months."

"Very good! Do this exercise with your lead, and when you meet with your manager, you may just update him about your conversation with the lead so that he is aware," I explained.

"This seems like cheating. I thought I can get the promotion by using the technique but it is going to bring more work for me. Don't you have a magic wand. I will just turn that around my manager and get a letter of promotion," Siddharth said with sheepish smile.

We all laughed at Siddharth's comment but Anuj soon turned thoughtful.

Treat your boss as buddy

TELL ME MY
DEVOTEE
WHAT DO YOU
WANT?
NANDA

6 6 I feel you are underestimating a manager. He knows everything, he can do anything he wants, he is all powerful," Anuj said.

Siddharth suddenly stood straight raising one of his hand with open palm towards Anuj like a god's posture and said loudly, "Tell me my devotee what do you want, I will grant you anything you wish for. I am your manager"

Suddenly from nowhere a stray dog came running towards Siddharth and started barking. Siddharth got scared a bit and sat down. We all laughed loudly at Siddharth's enactment.

"Understanding of manager as a superhuman is one of the biggest reason why we see so many people in corporate world getting stuck in their career," I said.

"In this entire process of managing your manager, consider your manager just another person with human emotions. Your manager has the same needs as yours. He or she also needs career growth and success in life. Any opportunity to help achieve his or her goals will be much appreciated. Do not offer any material assistance unless you would do the same to one of your colleagues, but if an occasion to help arises, then do not hesitate in doing so as you would to any of your colleagues.

Feed your manager's intellect, not his or her ego

"Just as you need appreciation for every work you have done well, your manager also needs such input. If you find your manager has done something right for you or your team or in any area, then appreciate him or her on the first occasion that presents itself. But this must be done in private.

"While doing so, ensure that you specify the commendable act so that it does not feed your manager's ego but his or her intellect. Keep track of your manager's good deeds and behaviors so that you can sincerely give him or her proper recognition.

"Similarly, if you find that your manager did wrong, then provide feedback on the specific instance. Mention what action would have been more appropriate for the team or the company so that he or she will be able to understand the context better. In this entire process, obtain his or her permission before giving feedback. Sometimes, people are not in the right frame of mind. If you are not careful, then it may work against you. But it is essential to offer feedback so that your manager finds you as an intellectual partner, not just another employee who only wants favors for career progression.

"Set healthy boundaries. It is easy to fall into the trap of thinking that your boss wants 100% of your every waking moment. However, setting reasonable boundaries shows that you are smart, know how to take care of yourself, and are willing to be assertive. Don't justify, rationalize, or apologize; just set boundaries calmly, firmly, and respectfully.

"Never make excuses. It's normal to want to get yourself off the hook, but the fact is that excuses don't work and make you look bad. At the end of the day, nobody cares about excuses. Minimize any damage done by being responsible and taking ownership of your problems as you work to do better.

"Make your boss look good. No one has ever made himself or herself great by putting down someone else. Especially if your boss is performing below par, do what you can to help shore up things. When you make your manager look good, you invest in a critical relationship and make yourself look even better in the process.

"Be a consistently positive force. Discipline yourself to seek what is beneficial in every situation. Think, speak, and act with positivity. When everyone else is complaining about an unreasonable restriction, find the workaround. It makes you a valuable team member and sets you apart.

"In short, treat your relationship with your manager as you would any other important relationship in your life. Invest time, energy, and creativity into making him or her happy, show your best self as much as possible, and create your own habits that cultivate trust," I explained.

"Sakti, you are too idealistic, I feel. There are evil managers who don't care what I do and say. They just want to get the result out of me and discard me when their job is done," Siddharth said.

"Yes, it seems that way many times. Despite all my suggestions, you may find your manager unreasonable and difficult to manage. If you consider your manager an entire package and the package is totally unacceptable, then you leave few avenues for change. It is important to understand what's wrong with your manager.

"First, determine whether your manager is the problem, not you. Before trying to fix your bad manager, make sure you are dealing with one. Is there a reason for the undesirable behavior, or are you too hard on him or her?

"Observe your manager for a few days, and try to notice how many tasks he or she does well versus poorly. When your manager is doing something 'bad,' try to imagine the most forgiving reason why it could have occurred. Is it truly his or her fault, or could it be something beyond his or her control?

"No matter how bad your manager's behavior is, avoid letting it affect your work. You want to stay on good terms with other leaders in the company (and keep your job!).

"Don't try to even the score by working slower or taking excessive 'mental health' days or longer lunches. It will only put you further behind in your workload and build a case for your boss to give you the old heave-ho before you're ready to go.

"If you still find yourself dealing with a conflict, give it some time before reacting. Timing is often everything when managing a conflict with a manager. Sometimes, it makes more sense to wait it out than confront the situation head on. If your boss has a lot on his or her plate this month, his or her stress level may be high, and he or she may not take as kindly to your issues.

"If your manager has anger management problems, identify what triggers his or her meltdowns and be extra militant about avoiding those.

"For example, if your manager flips when you miss a deadline, add an extra buffer and keep raising red flags if there are signs of delay. If your manager starts foaming at the mouth if you arrive a minute after 9 a.m., plan to get there at 8:45. Every. Single. Day.

"When dealing with a disagreement, pull out some techniques from couples' therapy to work through the issue. For instance, repeat what your boss says and ask, 'Is that what you meant?' If he or she agrees with your recap, ask him or her to tell you more about it. When you echo someone's perspective, you give him or her a chance to expound and crucially, to feel heard.

"When dealing with an incompetent manager, sometimes it's best to make some leadership decisions on your own.

"If you know your field well enough, there is no reason not to go ahead with creating and pursuing a direction that you know will achieve success for your company. People who do so are followed by their peers as natural leaders. The management, although maybe not your direct boss, will notice your initiative. Of course, you don't want to do something that undermines your boss; keep him or her in the loop.

"Despite that, if you get an 'evil' manager as Siddharth said, and you don't find a way out and feel stuck, then it's time to look for an alternative. Your résumé will come handy as you have been preparing it throughout your career. Your presence in online social media will be useful as you have been demonstrating your skills on global platforms. Your constant effort in learning will help you obtain a new job. When interviewing with a new company, research about it ahead of time to make sure you're not getting into another situation with a less-than-ideal manager.

"Have coffee or lunch with one or more staff members in the new company. Ostensibly, your purpose is to learn general information about the business and its culture. However, use this opportunity to discover as much about your potential boss as possible, without appearing creepy," I said.

"So Sakti, have you used all these strategies over the past 20 years of your career?" Siddharth asked.

"Yes, mostly."

"Then why have you remained in the same position for more than five years now?"

"You mean designation."

"Correct."

"Because career growth doesn't necessarily mean designation change. It means increased power, corporate status, and confidence," I clarified.

Anuj and Siddharth looked thoughtful. It was almost noon by now. We returned to the city.